GET that GRIT

By: Marissa Tawney Thaler

Have you ever had a problem that seemed

TOO HUGE

to handle?

The shoe that just won't tie.

The bike you just can't ride.

Have you ever just wanted to say...

Well, I've got a feeling that you could use some GRIT.

What's GRIT? You've never heard of it?

GRIT is **Courage** to try again and **Confidence** to do your best!

Having GRIT isn't being perfect, but it is striving for excellence!

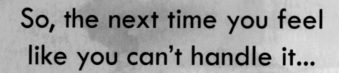

So, the next time you feel
like you can't handle it...

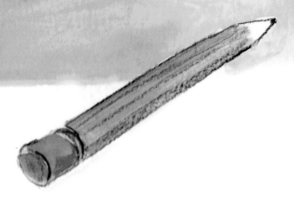

Scrunch up your face,

Make up your mind,

Nod your head, and...

And if you feel like throwing
in the towel...

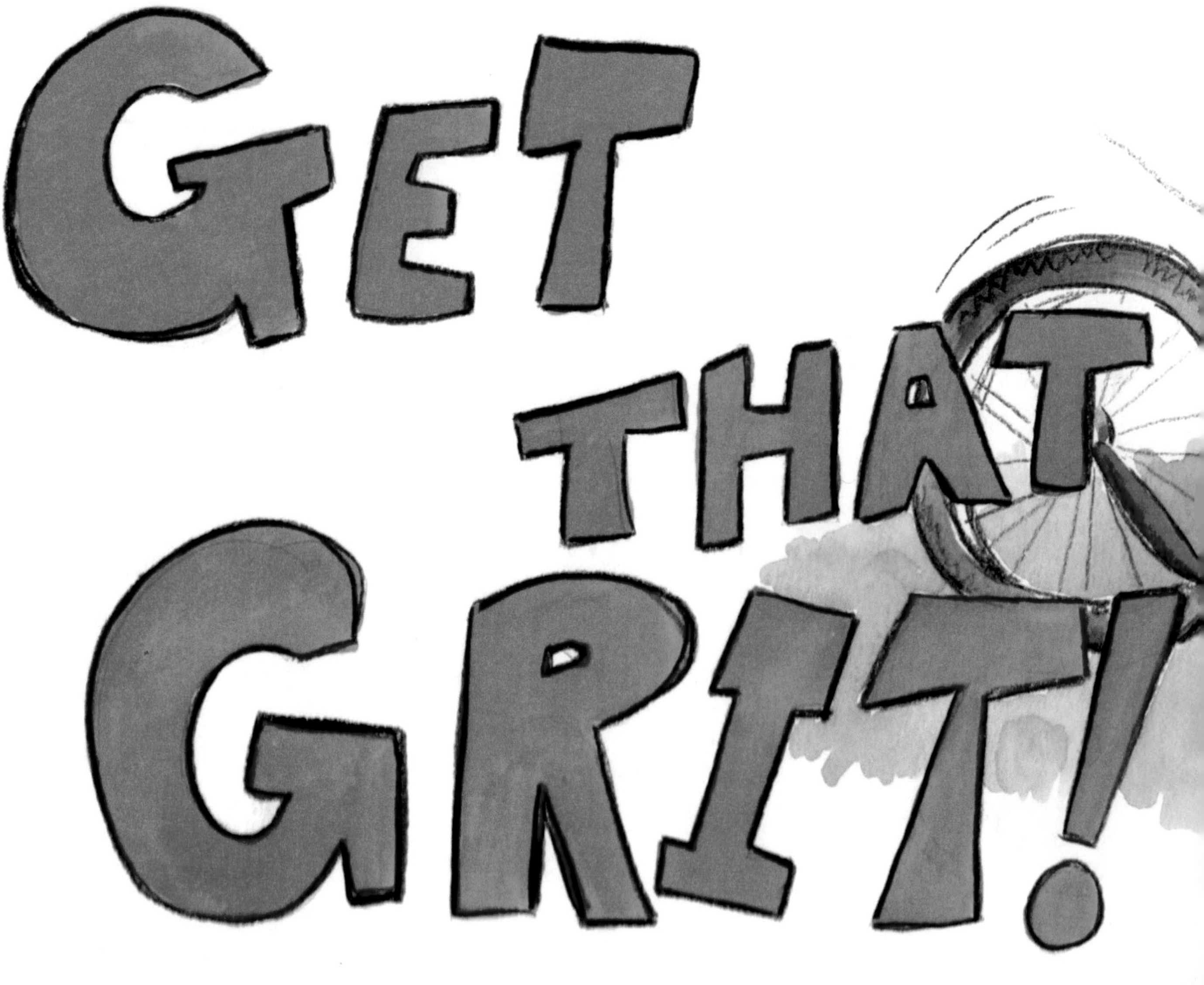
GET THAT GRIT!

When that
plate of broccoli is
just too high...

When
that room
is just too
dark...

When that book is just
too long...

And when you get good at persevering
through the little things,
you can get through the big
things, too.

Going to a new school
can be really scary.

Sticking up for a friend and telling the truth can be hard, too.

But you know what to do!

Made in the USA
Lexington, KY
15 November 2019

57098006R00021